STORY GEMS

OWAIS FAROOQ

Made with ♥ on the Notion Press Platform
www.notionpress.com

This book is dedicated to all the dreamers and believers out there. May this story inspire you to chase your own passions and never give up on your own journey. Thank you to my family and friends for their unwavering support and encouragement throughout the writing process. And to the readers, thank you for joining me on this adventure.This book is dedicated to all the dreamers and believers out there. May this story inspire you to chase your own passions and never give up on your own journey. Thank you to my family and friends for their unwavering support and encouragement throughout the writing process. And to the readers, thank you for joining me on this adventure.This book is dedicated to all the dreamers and believers out there. May this story inspire you to chase your own passions and never give up on your own journey. Thank you to my family and friends for their unwavering support and encouragement throughout the writing process. And to the readers, thank you for joining me on this adventure.This book is dedicated to all the dreamers and believers out there. May this story inspire you to chase your own passions and never give up on your own journey. Thank you to my family and friends for their unwavering support and encouragement throughout the writing process. And to the readers, thank you for joining me on this adventure.This book is dedicated to all the dreamers and believers out there. May this story inspire you to chase your own passions and never give up on your own journey. Thank you to my family and friends for their unwavering support and encouragement throughout the writing process. And to the readers, thank you for joining me on this adventure.This book is dedicated to all the dreamers and believers out there. May this story inspire you to chase your own passions and never give up on your own journey. Thank you to my family and friends for their unwavering support and encouragement throughout the writing process. And to the readers, thank you for joining me on this adventure.This book is dedicated to all the dreamers and believers out there. May this story inspire you to chase your own passions and never give up on your own journey. Thank you to my family and friends for their unwavering support and encouragement throughout the writing process. And to the readers, thank you for joining me on this adventure.This book is dedicated to all the dreamers and believers out there. May this story inspire you to chase your own passions and never give up on your own journey. Thank you to my family and friends for their unwavering support and encouragement throughout the writing process. And to the readers, thank you for joining me on this adventure.

Contents

Foreword

It is my great pleasure to introduce this book, which is the result of the author's creativity, imagination, and hard work. The story you are about to read takes you on a journey through the lives of its characters, exploring their joys, sorrows, struggles, and triumphs. It's a story that is sure to entertain, inspire, and touch your heart.

At the heart of this book is a message about the power of perseverance, the importance of kindness, and the value of friendship. As you turn the pages and immerse yourself in the story, I hope you'll find yourself transported to a world where anything is possible and where the human spirit can overcome even the greatest obstacles.

The author has poured their heart and soul into this book, and I'm sure you'll agree that their dedication and passion shine through on every page. So sit back, relax, and let yourself be carried away by the magic of this wonderful story. Enjoy!

Preface

I have always loved stories. As a child, I would spend hours lost in the pages of books, transported to different worlds and experiencing adventures through the eyes of my favorite characters. And now, as an adult, I still find that same joy and wonder in the art of storytelling.

This book is the product of my own imagination and the countless hours I've spent honing my craft as a writer. It's a story that has been with me for a long time, and one that I'm excited to share with the world.

At its core, this is a story about the power of human connection. It's about the bonds we form with others, the challenges we face together, and the ways in which those experiences shape us and change us for the better.

But it's also a story about the magic of the world around us, and the ways in which even the most ordinary moments can be transformed into something extraordinary.

I hope that as you read this book, you'll find yourself drawn into the lives of its characters and swept up in their journey. I hope that you'll laugh, cry, and feel your heart swell with emotion as their story unfolds.

Above all, I hope that this book inspires you to find the magic in your own life, and to seek out those connections and experiences that make it truly meaningful.

Thank you for choosing to spend your time with this book. I hope you enjoy it as much as I enjoyed writing it.

Acknowledgements

Writing a book is a solitary endeavor, but it's not a journey one can undertake entirely alone. There are many people who helped me along the way, and I want to express my gratitude to them.

First and foremost, I want to thank my family and friends for their unwavering support and encouragement. Their belief in me and my writing gave me the motivation to keep going, even when the writing process was tough.

I also want to thank my fellow writers who offered feedback, encouragement, and a listening ear when I needed it. Their support meant the world to me.

Lastly, I want to thank the readers of this book. You are the reason I wrote this story, and I'm so grateful to have the opportunity to share it with you.

Thank you all for your support, your encouragement, and your belief in me and my writing.

Prologue

The city had always been a place of light and noise, its streets filled with people and its buildings stretching high into the sky. But as night fell and the crowds dwindled, a different kind of energy began to emerge.

In the darkness, the city became a place of mystery and secrets. It was a time when anything could happen, when the impossible seemed suddenly within reach.

And it was on one of these nights that our story begins.

In the heart of the city, there was a small cafe tucked away in an alley. It was a place where the coffee was strong, the music was soft, and the conversation was always lively.

And it was there, in that cozy little cafe, that two people met. They were strangers at first, each lost in their own thoughts and their own lives. But as the night wore on and the coffee flowed, they began to talk.

They talked about their hopes and dreams, their fears and regrets. They talked about the world around them, and about the secrets they kept hidden inside.

And as they talked, something magical began to happen. The cafe faded away, and the city with it. They were no longer strangers in a crowded city, but two people sharing a moment of connection, of understanding, of true human connection.

This is the story of that night, and the many nights that followed. It's a story of friendship, of love, of hope, and of the magic that can be found in the most unexpected places. So come with me, and let's journey together into the heart of the city, where anything is possible and anything can happen.

CHAPTER ONE

THE LOST KEY

Sophie had always loved exploring her grandmother's attic. There was something magical about the dusty old boxes and forgotten treasures that lay hidden up there, waiting to be discovered. But one day, as she was rummaging through a particularly old and musty trunk, she found something that would change her life forever.

It was a small silver key, intricately carved and rusted with age. Sophie had no idea what it opened, but she knew it was important. She asked her grandmother about it, but she just shrugged and said she couldn't remember. It was as if the key had always been there, a forgotten relic of a time long gone.

Determined to find out what the key unlocked, Sophie searched the entire house from top to bottom. She checked every door, every drawer, every cabinet, but nothing seemed to fit. As days turned into weeks, she began to lose hope that she would ever solve the mystery.

But then, one stormy night, she heard a strange sound coming from the attic. It was a soft tinkling, like the sound of something metal falling onto a hard surface. She crept up the creaky stairs, heart pounding with anticipation.

And there it was: a small wooden chest, sitting in the middle of the attic floor. The keyhole on the front of the chest glinted in the dim light, and Sophie knew without a doubt that this was what the key had been meant for.

With trembling hands, she inserted the key and turned it. The lock clicked open, and she slowly lifted the lid. Inside was a single sheet of paper, covered in an elegant script that she could barely read.

It was a letter, written by her great-grandmother to her grandmother, explaining the true history of the family and the secret they had kept hidden for generations. As Sophie read the letter, she realized that the key and the chest had been waiting for her all along, to uncover the truth and carry on the legacy of her family.

CHAPTER TWO

THE FINAL GAME

For years, the world had been waiting for the ultimate showdown between the two greatest chess players of all time: Robert Fischer and Anatoly Karpov. The stakes were high, with millions of dollars and the honor of being crowned the greatest chess player in history on the line.

The game was held in a grand hall in the heart of Moscow, with hundreds of spectators from around the world watching in anticipation. As the two players took their seats across from each other, the room fell silent.

The game began, and it quickly became clear that this was no ordinary match. Each move was calculated, each piece carefully placed. The tension in the room was palpable as the game dragged on, with neither player willing to make a mistake.

As the hours turned into days, the world watched in awe as Fischer and Karpov battled it out. The media was in a frenzy, with live coverage of the game being broadcast around the clock.

Finally, on the third day of the game, Fischer made a daring move that caught Karpov off guard. The audience erupted in cheers as they realized that Fischer was about to win.

But then, something strange happened. Fischer hesitated, his hand trembling as he reached for the piece that would seal his victory. He looked up at Karpov, who was staring back at him with a strange expression on his face.

And then, in an instant, everything changed. Fischer's eyes rolled back in his head, and he collapsed onto the table.

The room was in chaos as the medics rushed to his side, but it was too late. Fischer was dead, his final move forever lost to the world.

As the investigation into Fischer's death began, rumors began to circulate that he had been poisoned by one of Karpov's supporters. But the truth was far stranger than anyone could have imagined.

It was discovered that Fischer had been suffering from a rare neurological disorder, and that the stress of the final game had triggered a fatal seizure. The chess world was in shock, and the game would forever be remembered as the Final Game.

CHAPTER THREE

THE BROKEN PROMISE

Emily had always been close to her grandfather. They would spend hours together, playing games, telling stories, and laughing. He had promised her that they would always be together, no matter what happened.

But then, one day, he was gone. Emily was heartbroken, and she couldn't understand why her grandfather had broken his promise.

Years went by, and Emily grew up. She went to college, got a job, and started a family of her own. But no matter how busy she was, she never forgot her grandfather and the promise he had made to her.

One day, as she was cleaning out her attic, she found a box filled with old photographs and letters. As she sorted through them, she came across a letter that her grandfather had written to her before he died.

In the letter, he explained that he had been diagnosed with a terminal illness and that he had known that he would not be able to keep his promise to her. He had written the letter to tell her how much he loved her and to explain why he had broken his promise.

Emily was devastated, but also grateful to finally understand why her grandfather had left her. She realized that life was full of broken promises, but that it was up to her to keep her own promises to the people she loved.

She made a promise to herself that day, to live her life with purpose and to always cherish the memories of her grandfather. And as she looked at the old photographs and letters, she felt a sense of peace and comfort, knowing that her grandfather was still with her, in her heart and in her memories.

CHAPTER FOUR

THE SILENT STRANGER

As the town of Willow Creek prepared for the annual Harvest Festival, a stranger arrived on the outskirts of town. He was a tall, lean man with weathered skin and piercing blue eyes. He carried a backpack and a guitar, and he said nothing to anyone as he walked through the streets.

The townspeople were curious about the stranger, but also a bit afraid. They had heard stories of travelers who brought trouble and danger with them, and they wondered what this silent stranger might bring.

As the festival began, the stranger made his way to the town square. He sat down on a bench and pulled out his guitar, strumming a few chords before launching into a song. His voice was haunting and beautiful, and the melody drifted through the air like a gentle breeze.

The townspeople were mesmerized by the stranger's performance, and they gathered around him, listening intently. When he finished playing, they applauded, and someone asked him his name.

The stranger didn't answer, but simply smiled and began to play another song. And so it went for the rest of the day, with the stranger playing one song after another, captivating the audience with his music.

As the sun began to set, the stranger packed up his guitar and prepared to leave. The townspeople gathered around him, asking him to stay, but he shook his head and began to walk away.

Suddenly, a young girl ran up to him and handed him a piece of paper. "Please come back," she said. "We need your music."

The stranger looked at the girl and then at the piece of paper. It was an invitation to play at the local coffee shop, and the girl had written a note begging him to come.

The stranger smiled and nodded, and the townspeople erupted in cheers. They followed him to the coffee shop, where he played for hours, filling the room with his beautiful music.

And from that day on, the stranger became a beloved fixture in the town of Willow Creek. He played at the coffee shop every week, and people came from miles around to hear him play. Though he never spoke a word, his music spoke volumes, bringing joy and healing to all who heard it.

CHAPTER FIVE

THE HIDDEN TREASURE

In the small town of Oakwood, nestled in the heart of the countryside, there was a legend of a hidden treasure. According to the town's elders, a wealthy merchant named William had buried a chest full of gold coins and precious jewels somewhere in the town before he passed away.

The story of the treasure had been passed down from generation to generation, and many had searched for it, but nobody had ever found it. It had become somewhat of a local obsession, with people still searching for it to this day.

One day, a young man named Jack arrived in Oakwood. He had heard about the legend of the hidden treasure and was determined to find it. Jack was a keen treasure hunter and had spent many years exploring ancient ruins and lost cities.

He began his search by talking to the locals, trying to gather as much information as he could. Many were reluctant to speak about the treasure, believing it to be a fool's errand. But eventually, Jack managed to find an old man who claimed to know the location of the hidden treasure.

The old man, who was named George, took Jack to a secluded spot on the outskirts of town. He pointed to an old oak tree and said, "The treasure is buried beneath this tree."

Jack was ecstatic, but he knew that he couldn't just start digging under the tree. He needed to be sure that the treasure was there before he started digging. He spent the next few days researching the history of the town and the merchant William.

Eventually, Jack discovered an old map of the town that showed the location of William's house. He went to the site and began to search for any clues that would lead him to the treasure. After hours of searching, Jack found an old diary that belonged to William.

The diary revealed that the treasure was indeed buried under the oak tree that George had pointed out. But William had left a clue for anyone who was brave enough to search for it. The clue read, "The treasure lies beneath the roots of the oak tree, where the sun first shines on the morning of the summer solstice."

Jack realized that he only had a few weeks to wait until the summer solstice. He spent the next few weeks studying the sun's path and the location of the oak tree. Finally, the day of the solstice arrived, and Jack was ready.

He arrived at the oak tree just as the sun began to rise. He started to dig, and after a few minutes, he felt something hard. He dug a little deeper and found a wooden chest. Jack opened the chest and couldn't believe his eyes. It was full of gold coins, diamonds, and rubies.

Jack had found the hidden treasure, and he knew that he would never have to worry about money again. He left Oakwood that same day, a wealthy man, but he knew that he would never forget the adventure that had led him to the treasure. And he hoped that one day, someone else would have the same adventure and find the treasure for themselves.

CHAPTER SIX

THE SECRET GARDEN

Once upon a time, in the English countryside, there lived a young girl named Mary Lennox. Mary had grown up in India, but after her parents died, she was sent to live with her uncle, Archibald Craven, in his large mansion on the Yorkshire moors.

Mary was a spoiled and sickly child who had never known love or affection. She was used to having servants wait on her hand and foot and had no interest in making friends or exploring the world around her.

But everything changed when Mary discovered a secret garden on the grounds of her uncle's estate. The garden had been locked up for ten years since Archibald's wife, Lily, had died. The garden had been her favorite place, and after she passed away, Archibald had locked it up and thrown away the key.

One day, while exploring the mansion, Mary met a friendly robin who led her to the hidden key to the garden. Mary was overjoyed to find a place of her own, and with the help of a young servant boy named Dickon, she began to restore the garden to its former beauty.

As Mary worked in the garden, she became healthier and happier. She learned about the plants and the animals that lived there and began to form a deep connection with nature. Mary's transformation didn't go unnoticed, and even her uncle, who had always been distant and cold, began to take an interest in her.

As Mary worked on the garden, she discovered the door to an even more secret part of the garden that had been completely neglected for years. She found out that her cousin Colin, who was sickly and bedridden, had been hidden away in the mansion's rooms for his whole life because his father believed he was too weak to live.

Mary befriended Colin and told him about the garden, and together they began to imagine the garden as a magical place where they could be healed. They even came up with a plan to sneak Colin out of his room and bring him to the garden, where he could get some fresh air and sunshine.

When Colin finally saw the garden, he was overwhelmed with emotion. He realized that he had been missing out on the beauty of the world because of his father's fear. Colin and Mary's uncle, Archibald, came to the garden, and they were all reunited as a family.

The secret garden had not only brought Mary and Colin together but had also healed their family's wounds. The garden had become a symbol of love, hope, and transformation, and Mary and Colin had learned that with a little bit of magic and a lot of hard work, anything was possible.

CHAPTER SEVEN

THE CURSED MIRROR

Once upon a time, there was a beautiful princess named Isabella who lived in a grand palace. She was known for her stunning beauty and her kind heart, but she was also vain and loved to admire herself in the mirror. She spent hours staring at herself, combing her hair, and applying makeup. One day, a mysterious woman appeared at the palace gates and offered Isabella a magnificent mirror made of gold and decorated with precious gems. The woman warned Isabella that the mirror was cursed and that it had the power to show her the ugliness within her heart if she used it for vanity. Isabella didn't believe in curses and eagerly accepted the mirror. She placed it in her room and began admiring herself even more. However, as time went on, Isabella started to notice changes in her appearance when she looked into the mirror. Her skin became pallid, and her eyes became sunken. Isabella tried to ignore the changes and continued to use the mirror, but her vanity had taken over her, and she became cruel and selfish. She became obsessed with her beauty and didn't care about anyone else's needs. She treated her servants and the people of the kingdom with contempt, and her cruelty spread throughout the palace. One day, Isabella looked into the cursed mirror and was shocked to see a hideous monster staring back at her. She realized that the curse had taken hold of her and that the mirror had shown her the ugliness of her heart. She begged for forgiveness and promised to change her ways, but it was too late. The curse had already taken its toll, and Isabella's once-beautiful face was now twisted and deformed. She tried to remove the curse, but it was too powerful, and she was doomed to live the rest of her life with the cursed mirror as her only reflection. The people of the kingdom shunned Isabella and feared her, believing that her curse was contagious. Isabella was banished to the highest tower of the palace, where she spent the rest of her days staring into the cursed mirror, tormented by her reflection.

Years passed, and the people of the kingdom forgot about Isabella and her curse. The palace fell into disrepair, and the kingdom was no longer the prosperous and happy place it once was.

One day, a young girl named Emily stumbled upon the old palace. She was fascinated by its grandeur and the stories she had heard of the princess who had been cursed. Emily was a curious and kind-hearted girl, and she felt drawn to the palace and the secrets it held.

As she explored the palace, Emily heard whispers of a cursed princess who still lived in the highest tower. She was determined to uncover the truth and climbed up the winding staircase to the top of the tower.

When Emily reached the top, she found Isabella still staring into the cursed mirror. Emily was shocked to see the once-beautiful princess now twisted and deformed, but she felt a deep sense of compassion for her.

Emily spoke to Isabella and listened to her story. She could see the remorse in Isabella's eyes and knew that she had been punished enough for her vanity and cruelty.

Emily realized that she had the power to break the curse and restore Isabella's beauty.

With determination, Emily took the cursed mirror and smashed it to pieces. The curse was lifted, and Isabella was restored to her former beauty. She was overwhelmed with gratitude and begged Emily for forgiveness.

Emily forgave Isabella and showed her kindness and compassion, teaching her to be humble and care for others. Isabella learned from her mistakes and dedicated her life to serving the people of the kingdom and making amends for her past behavior.

The kingdom was restored to its former glory, and the people rejoiced at the return of their beloved princess. Emily was hailed as a hero, and her kindness and compassion had saved the kingdom from darkness and despair. Isabella and Emily became lifelong friends, and their story inspired generations to come.

CHAPTER EIGHT

FORGOTTEN FOREST

Once there was a lush forest at the edge of a small village. It was a place of wonder and mystery, filled with towering trees, babbling brooks, and all manner of woodland creatures. The villagers would often venture into the forest to gather firewood or hunt for food, and they felt a deep connection to the ancient trees and the earthy scent of the forest floor. But over time, the villagers began to take the forest for granted. They chopped down trees for their own needs, left trash behind, and hunted animals to extinction. The forest began to suffer, and its once-bustling ecosystem dwindled. As the years passed, the villagers forgot about the forest. They no longer visited its peaceful glades or marveled at its natural wonders. The forest became a distant memory, and the villagers went about their daily lives without a second thought. One day, a young girl named Lily stumbled upon the forgotten forest. She had been exploring the countryside and had lost her way, but as she wandered deeper into the forest, she felt a strange sense of comfort. The rustling of leaves and the chirping of birds seemed to speak to her in a language she could understand. Lily spent hours exploring the forest, taking in its beauty and feeling a sense of wonder and awe she had never experienced before. She found a small waterfall and a clearing where a family of deer grazed. She even discovered a hidden cave filled with glowing mushrooms and sparkling crystals. Over time, Lily began to visit the forest every day. She would sit by the waterfall and read a book or watch the deer from a distance.

She would marvel at the changing colors of the leaves in autumn and the blooming of wildflowers in spring. She felt a deep sense of connection to the forest, and it became her sanctuary from the stresses of daily life.

As Lily spent more time in the forest, she began to notice something strange. The animals seemed to be disappearing. She saw fewer and fewer deer in the clearing, and the birdsong that once filled the air was now scarce.

Lily realized that the forest was in trouble, and she knew she had to do something to help. She began to research ways to restore the forest's ecosystem and enlisted the help of the villagers.

At first, many of the villagers were hesitant to listen to Lily's plea. They had long forgotten the beauty and importance of the forest and saw it only as a resource to exploit. But Lily persisted, organizing community clean-up days and advocating for sustainable harvesting practices.

Slowly but surely, the forest began to recover. The animals returned, and the trees began to grow back. The villagers began to see the forest as more than just a source of material goods, but as a living, breathing entity that needed their protection and care.

As the forest flourished, so did the community. The villagers began to take pride in their stewardship of the land, and the sense of connection that had been lost was restored. And Lily, who had once been lost herself, found a sense of purpose and belonging in the forest that had become her home.

CHAPTER NINE

THE HAUNTED DOLL

Once there was a beautiful antique doll named Victoria, who had been passed down through generations of a wealthy family. She had been treasured by each owner and had lived a long life of luxury and care. But one day, something changed.

The current owner, a young girl named Emily, began to notice strange occurrences in her room at night. Her toys would be moved, and her clothes would be rearranged. Emily felt uneasy, but she could not figure out what was happening.

One night, as Emily was trying to sleep, she heard a faint whispering. It sounded like a child's voice, but it was coming from her doll Victoria. Emily was scared, but she tried to ignore it, thinking that she was just imagining things.

The strange happenings continued, and Emily's fear grew. She tried to tell her parents, but they did not believe her. They thought that she was just having nightmares.

One night, as Emily was tossing and turning, she saw a shadowy figure appear next to her bed. It was the figure of a little girl, but she was completely black, like a silhouette. Emily could not see any details, but she knew that it was Victoria.

The figure began to move towards Emily, and she felt a cold breeze on her face. She screamed, but the figure did not stop. It came closer and closer, until it was right in front of her.

Suddenly, the figure vanished, and Victoria was sitting in her place. Emily was terrified, but she knew that she had to find out what was happening.

She decided to do some research and discovered that Victoria had a dark history. The previous owner had been a young girl who had died in a tragic accident, and Victoria had been with her at the time.

Emily realized that Victoria was haunted by the girl's spirit and decided to take action. She called in a paranormal investigator, who was able to perform a cleansing ritual on the doll.

After the cleansing, the strange occurrences stopped, and Emily was finally able to sleep peacefully. Victoria remained in her room, but she was no longer a source of fear. Emily had a newfound respect for the doll and the history that she carried with her.

From that day on, Emily made sure to treat all of her toys with care and respect, knowing that they might have stories and histories that she could not see. She learned that even the most innocent-looking objects could have a dark side, and she vowed to always be aware of that.

CHAPTER TEN

THE LAST DANCE

It was the night of the annual ball, and everyone in the small town was getting ready for the event of the year. The decorations were up, the music was playing, and the guests were arriving in their finest attire. For many, it was a night to remember, but for one woman, it would be her last dance.

Eleanor had been looking forward to the ball for months. She had spent weeks choosing the perfect dress, getting her hair styled, and practicing her dance moves. She arrived at the ballroom with a sense of excitement and anticipation, eager to enjoy the festivities and dance the night away.

As she entered the ballroom, Eleanor was struck by the beauty of the scene before her. The room was filled with glittering chandeliers, sparkling decorations, and couples swaying to the music. She saw familiar faces and exchanged greetings with old friends, feeling a sense of warmth and belonging.

But as the night wore on, Eleanor began to feel a sense of unease. She noticed that there was one woman in particular who seemed to be watching her, a woman with dark hair and a strange intensity in her gaze. At first, Eleanor tried to ignore the woman's stare, but as the night went on, she couldn't help but feel a growing sense of discomfort.

As the music shifted to a slow, romantic tune, Eleanor was approached by a man who asked her to dance. She accepted, grateful for the distraction from the strange woman's gaze. They began to sway to the music, lost in the moment, when suddenly, Eleanor felt a sharp pain in her side.

She gasped and stumbled, feeling dizzy and disoriented. The man caught her as she fell, but it was too late. Eleanor realized with horror that she had been stabbed, and that the woman with the intense gaze was nowhere to be seen.

As the room erupted in chaos and confusion, Eleanor felt herself slipping away. She knew that she was dying, but she refused to let go. She clung to the memory of the beautiful ballroom, the music, and the sense of belonging she had felt. She thought of all the dances she had shared with her friends and loved ones, and she wished desperately that she could have just one more.

As her vision began to fade, Eleanor saw a figure emerge from the shadows. It was the woman with the intense gaze, but now Eleanor could see that she was holding something in her hand, something small and glittering. The woman knelt beside Eleanor and placed the object in her hand, whispering something in her ear before disappearing into the night.

Eleanor's last dance had ended in tragedy, but as she slipped away, she clung to the small object in her hand, a precious reminder of the beauty and joy she had experienced that night. Her memory would live on, and her spirit would forever be a part of the magical world of the ballroom, where dreams come true and love never dies.

CHAPTER ELEVEN

THE MYSTERIOUS PAKAGE

It was a typical Monday morning when a mysterious package arrived at the doorstep of Emma's small apartment. She had no idea who sent it or what could be inside. Emma was a curious person by nature, and her curiosity was piqued by the package's arrival. She eagerly tore open the brown paper wrapping to reveal a small wooden box. As she opened the box, a strange feeling overcame her, as if something wasn't quite right. She shook it off and peered inside, finding a letter and a small key. The letter was written in elegant cursive and began with the words: "My dearest Emma, if you are reading this, I am no longer with you. I have left you a gift, a key to a place where we shared many memories. Go there and you will understand." Emma was bewildered by the letter. She had no idea who could have sent it or what place the letter was referring to. The only clue she had was the small key that lay in her hand. It was old and rusty, as if it had been lying dormant for years. Emma decided to do some research to try and uncover the mystery of the package. She scoured old photo albums, searching for any clues that might help her understand what the letter was talking about. After hours of searching, she finally found an old picture of her and her late grandmother, who had passed away many years ago. They were standing in front of a small wooden cabin in the woods, and Emma instantly recognized the background as the place the letter was referring to. Determined to uncover the truth, Emma set out to the cabin in the woods, holding the key tightly in her hand. As she walked through the dense forest, she began to feel a sense of unease. It was as if she was being watched, and every rustling of the leaves made her jump. But her determination to uncover the mystery kept her going. Finally, after what seemed like hours of walking, Emma arrived at the small wooden cabin. It was old and dilapidated, with vines growing up the sides and the door hanging off its hinges. Emma pushed the door open and stepped inside, holding her breath. The inside of the cabin was dark and musty, with cobwebs covering every surface. Emma searched the dusty corners of the cabin until she finally found what she was looking for. It was an old diary, written in her grandmother's hand. As Emma read through the diary, she uncovered the truth behind the mysterious package. Her grandmother had always been a mysterious woman, and she had led a life full of adventure and intrigue. In the diary, she described a hidden treasure that she had buried deep in the woods,

and she had left a key to the treasure with Emma's mother, to be passed down to Emma when the time was right.

Emma's heart raced as she read the words in her grandmother's diary. Could it be possible that the key she had received was the key to this hidden treasure? She quickly flipped through the pages, searching for any clues as to where it might be buried.

As she read on, Emma learned that her grandmother had hidden the treasure in a small clearing in the woods, not far from the cabin. She described the location in detail, and Emma realized that she had passed by the clearing on her way to the cabin.

Excitement coursing through her veins, Emma raced out of the cabin and back into the woods, determined to find the treasure her grandmother had left for her. She followed the directions in the diary, and before long, she came upon the small clearing her grandmother had described.

There, buried beneath a pile of leaves and dirt, Emma found a small chest. She eagerly unlocked it with the key and lifted the lid. Inside, she found a collection of old coins and jewelry, along with a note from her grandmother.

As Emma read the note, tears welled up in her eyes. Her grandmother had left her the treasure as a symbol of their special bond and the adventures they had shared. She hoped that Emma would continue to live a life full of adventure and curiosity, just as she had.

With a newfound sense of purpose, Emma left the woods and returned to her small apartment, clutching the treasure her grandmother had left her. From that day on, she made a promise to herself to live a life full of adventure, just like her grandmother had. And every time she looked at the treasure, she was reminded of the special bond they shared and the mysteries that awaited her in the world.

CHAPTER TWELVE

THE SECRET TUNNEL

Once upon a time, in a small village, nestled in the rolling hills, there was a secret tunnel. The tunnel had been carved out of the earth many years ago by a group of ancient craftsmen who had been tasked with creating a secret passageway between two neighboring kingdoms.

Over time, the kingdoms had fallen into conflict, and the tunnel was forgotten. The entrance had been sealed off and covered with earth and rocks, and it was only a matter of time before the tunnel was lost to history.

Many years later, a young boy named Jacob was exploring the woods near his home when he stumbled upon the entrance to the tunnel. At first, he thought it was just a cave, but as he got closer, he could see that there was a small, carved stone door.

Curiosity getting the better of him, Jacob pushed on the door, and to his surprise, it opened. He peered inside and saw that the tunnel was long and dark, with a faint light glowing at the other end. Jacob's heart pounded with excitement and fear as he stepped inside.

As he walked deeper into the tunnel, he could see that it was lined with intricate carvings and symbols, and the air was filled with the scent of ancient herbs and spices. After what seemed like hours of walking, Jacob finally emerged on the other side.

To his amazement, he found himself standing in a lush, green valley, surrounded by mountains and forests. It was a place he had never seen before, and yet it felt strangely familiar. As he looked around, he noticed that there were people milling about, going about their daily lives.

Jacob approached one of the villagers and asked where he was. The villager looked at him strangely and replied, "Why, you're in the Kingdom of Zanara, of course."

Jacob was stunned. He had never heard of this kingdom before, and yet here he was, standing in the middle of it. Over the next few days, he explored the kingdom, marveling at the sights and sounds he encountered. The people were friendly and welcoming, and he quickly made friends with many of them.

But as time passed, Jacob began to feel homesick. He missed his family and friends and longed to return home. He knew he couldn't stay in Zanara forever, but he didn't know how to get back to his own village.

One day, as he was wandering through the market, he overheard two merchants talking about a secret tunnel that ran between the two kingdoms. It was said that the entrance was hidden somewhere in the forest, and only those who knew its location could find it.

Jacob's heart leapt with excitement. Could this be the tunnel that he had used to enter Zanara? He approached the merchants and asked them about the tunnel. They looked at him skeptically, but finally relented and told him what they knew.

Jacob spent the next few weeks searching the forest for the entrance to the tunnel. He combed every inch of the woods, searching for any sign of the tunnel. Finally, one day, he stumbled upon a small, hidden entrance, just as the merchants had described.

With a sense of excitement and trepidation, Jacob stepped inside the tunnel and began the long journey back to his village. The journey was long and arduous, and at times he feared he would never make it back.

But finally, after what seemed like an eternity, he emerged from the tunnel and saw the familiar hills and fields of his village stretching out before him. He ran to his home, eager to tell his family and friends about his amazing adventure.

From that day forward, Jacob never forgot the secret tunnel that had led him to a magical world beyond his wildest dreams. And although he never returned to Z

CHAPTER THIRTEEN

THE STOLEN PAINTING

In the heart of the bustling city, there was a renowned art museum that housed some of the world's most treasured masterpieces. Among the collection was a stunning painting by a famous artist that had captivated the hearts of art enthusiasts for years. The painting was called "The Starry Night," and it was a masterpiece that was said to capture the beauty of the universe in a single stroke of the brush.

One fateful night, the museum was broken into by a group of thieves. They were determined to get their hands on "The Starry Night" and make it their own. Despite the best efforts of the museum's security team, the thieves managed to evade detection and make their way to the painting.

With practiced hands, they carefully removed the painting from its frame and made their escape. The theft was discovered the next morning, and the entire city was in an uproar. The museum offered a substantial reward for anyone who could provide information about the whereabouts of the painting.

As the days turned into weeks, the authorities searched high and low for any sign of the stolen painting. They interviewed suspects, scoured CCTV footage, and combed through evidence, but nothing seemed to lead them to the thieves or the painting.

Meanwhile, a young woman named Mia had just started her job as an assistant curator at the museum. She was an art lover at heart and was devastated by the theft of "The Starry Night." She spent her days pouring over the museum's collection, hoping to find any clues that might lead to the painting's recovery.

One day, while working in the museum's storage room, Mia noticed something odd about one of the paintings. She recognized it as a lesser-known work by the same artist who had painted "The Starry Night." Upon closer inspection, she realized that the painting had been tampered with. The signature had been altered, and the canvas had been stretched in an unusual way.

Mia's heart began to race as she realized that this could be a crucial piece of evidence. She immediately contacted the authorities and informed them of her discovery. After a thorough investigation, the painting was confirmed to be a fake, and the thieves were eventually tracked down and apprehended.

Thanks to Mia's keen eye and quick thinking, "The Starry Night" was recovered and returned to the museum, where it was placed back on display for all to see. Mia was hailed as a hero and was awarded a commendation for her role in the painting's recovery.

From that day forward, security at the museum was tightened, and "The Starry Night" was kept under closer watch to prevent any further attempts at theft. And Mia continued her work as an assistant curator, dedicated to preserving the beauty and history of the world's most treasured artworks.

CHAPTER FOURTEEN

THE DARK SECRET

In the small town of Cedar Creek, there was a house at the end of the street that had been abandoned for years. The windows were boarded up, the lawn was overgrown, and there was an eerie feeling that hung in the air around it. Most of the townspeople avoided the house altogether, but there were rumors that it held a dark secret.

The story went that the house had once belonged to a wealthy family who had mysteriously disappeared one night. No one knew what had happened to them, but some whispered that they had been involved in something sinister. Others said that the house was haunted by their restless spirits and that it was best to stay away.

Despite the warnings, a young couple named Emily and Ryan were drawn to the house's mysterious allure. They had recently moved to Cedar Creek and were looking for an adventure to embark on. They decided to investigate the abandoned house and see if they could uncover its secrets.

As they made their way through the overgrown lawn and up to the front door, they couldn't shake the feeling that they were being watched. The door creaked open, and they stepped inside, holding their breath as they waited for their eyes to adjust to the darkness.

The house was dusty and neglected, but there was a strange feeling in the air that made their hair stand on end. They made their way through the rooms, searching for any clues that might reveal the house's dark secret. They found old family photos, dusty books, and antique furniture, but nothing that seemed out of the ordinary.

As they were about to leave, Ryan noticed a door that was hidden behind a bookshelf. They moved the shelf aside and opened the door to reveal a narrow staircase that led down into the basement. Without a second thought, they descended the stairs, the darkness engulfing them.

In the basement, they found a room that was unlike any other in the house. It was pristine, with clean white walls and gleaming metal surfaces. In the center of the room was a large steel door with a combination lock.

Emily and Ryan's curiosity got the better of them, and they tried to crack the lock. After a few failed attempts, the lock clicked open, and the door swung open to reveal a hidden room.

The room was filled with strange, high-tech equipment that neither of them could identify. They found files filled with confidential documents, and photos of people they didn't recognize. It was clear that whatever had happened to the family that used to live in the house was far more sinister than anyone had suspected.

As they were about to leave, they heard footsteps coming from upstairs. They froze, realizing that they had been caught. They rushed back up the stairs and out the front door, leaving the house behind.

The next day, they returned to the house with the police, but the room in the basement was empty. The equipment and documents had been removed, leaving no trace of the dark secret that had been hidden within.

Emily and Ryan never spokc of thc housc again, but the memory of what they had discovered stayed with them. They couldn't shake the feeling that they had stumbled upon something truly sinister, and that the truth of what had happened in the house might never be revealed.

CHAPTER FIFTEEN

THE MYSTERY OF NEW OXFORD SCHOOL

CHAPTER SIXTEEN

THE SECRET LIFE OF TREES

In a world that grows increasingly disconnected from nature, one young girl is about to discover the hidden world of the forest. As she wanders through the woods, she can't help but feel that the trees have a secret life all their own.

One day, she stumbles upon a wise old oak tree that seems to be alive in a way that the others are not. She reaches out to touch its bark and feels a jolt of electricity run through her body. The tree seems to be communicating with her, sending her a message that she can't quite understand.

Determined to uncover the truth about the forest, the young girl sets out on a journey to learn everything she can about trees. She studies the different species, their growth patterns, and the ways they communicate with each other.

She learns that trees are not just silent witnesses to the world around them. They are active participants, constantly communicating with each other through a vast network of roots and fungi. They share nutrients, warn each other of danger, and even care for their young.

As she delves deeper into the secret life of trees, the girl begins to realize the extent of the damage humans have inflicted on the natural world. She sees the clearcut forests, the polluted rivers, and the dying coral reefs, and she knows that she must do something to help.

With the help of the wise old oak and the other trees of the forest, the young girl embarks on a mission to save the natural world. She starts by planting new trees, cleaning up litter, and spreading awareness about the importance of conservation.

As she works tirelessly to protect the forest, the girl begins to understand that the trees are not just a source of inspiration and wonder, but they are also her friends. They have welcomed her into their secret world and given her a new purpose in life.

In the end, the girl realizes that we are all connected to the natural world, and that it is up to each and every one of us to protect it. With the help of the trees, she has found her place in the world, and she knows that she will never be alone as long as they are by her side.

CHAPTER SEVENTEEN

The Disappearance of Emily White

Emily White was an ordinary girl living in a small town in the heart of the countryside. She had long brown hair that she wore in a braid and bright blue eyes that sparkled in the sunlight. Emily loved spending time outdoors, exploring the woods and playing with her friends. One day, Emily disappeared without a trace. Her family and friends searched the woods, the nearby river, and every inch of the town, but there was no sign of her. The police were called, and an investigation was launched, but they found no evidence of foul play. As time passed, people began to forget about Emily. Her family moved away, and her friends grew up and moved on with their lives. But one person never forgot about Emily: a young journalist named Sarah. Sarah had always been fascinated by the story of Emily's disappearance, and she had spent years researching the case. She had read every article, interviewed every witness, and pored over every piece of evidence. One day, Sarah received a tip from an anonymous source that led her to a small town on the outskirts of the city. She followed the lead, and it led her to an old farmhouse on the edge of town. As she approached the house, she could feel her heart racing. Something about the place didn't feel right. It was dark and quiet, and the only sound was the rustling of leaves in the wind. Sarah knocked on the door, but there was no answer. She tried the handle, and to her surprise, it was unlocked. She pushed the door open slowly and stepped inside. The house was old and musty, with cobwebs in every corner. The air was thick with dust, and Sarah coughed as she walked through the hallway. She searched every room, but there was no sign of anyone living there. As she turned to leave, Sarah noticed a trapdoor in the floor. She approached it cautiously, and as she lifted it, a gust of cold air rushed up at her. She shone her flashlight into the darkness below and saw a set of stairs leading down into the earth. Without thinking, Sarah descended the stairs. At the bottom, she found herself in a small room with concrete walls. There was a cot in the corner, a desk with a computer, and a pile of notebooks stacked neatly on a shelf. Sarah picked up one of the notebooks and began to read. As she flipped through the pages, her heart sank. The notebooks were full of notes on Emily White's life, her routines, and her habits. There were pictures of her, taken from a distance, and pages of detailed observations of her behavior. Sarah realized with a sick feeling in her stomach that she had stumbled upon the lair of Emily's kidnapper. She quickly made her way back up the stairs and out of the house, dialing the police as she went.

The police arrived shortly after Sarah made the call, and they searched the house thoroughly. They found evidence that confirmed their worst fears: Emily had indeed been kidnapped and held captive in the farmhouse.

The kidnapper was eventually identified as a man named John, who had been living off the grid for years. He had been watching Emily from a distance and had become obsessed with her. He had planned every detail of her kidnapping meticulously, and he had managed to keep her hidden away for years.

When Emily was found, she was malnourished and traumatized, but alive. She was taken to the hospital for treatment and eventually reunited with her family. It was a miracle that she had survived after all those years in captivity.

John was arrested and charged with kidnapping, imprisonment, and a slew of other charges. He was sentenced to life in prison, and Emily and her family were finally able to find closure after all those years.

As for Sarah, her investigative journalism had played a crucial role in bringing Emily home. She won several awards for her work and went on to become a successful journalist, always remembering the case that had changed her life.

The disappearance of Emily White had been a dark chapter in the town's history, but it had also shown the power of determination and perseverance in the face of tragedy. Emily had been lost, but she had been found, and justice had been served.

9 798890 022370

Printed by Libri Plureos GmbH in Hamburg,
Germany